A MAGIC BOOK

SASHA STEENSEN

Author Photo: Richard Hadfield

Cover Illustration: The Strobridge Lith. Co., Cincinnatti & New York /
Library of Congress, Prints and Photographs Division
[LC-USZC4-8001]

Published in the United States by   Fence Books
                                     303 East Eighth Street, #B1
                                     New York, NY 10009
                                     www.fencebooks.com

Book design by   Rebecca Wolff

Fence Books are distributed by   University Press of New England
                                     www.upne.com

and printed in Canada by   Westcan Printing Group
                                     www.westcanpg.com

Library of Congress Cataloguing in Publication Data
        Steensen, Sasha [1974–]
        A Magic Book / Sasha Steensen

Library of Congress Control Number: 2004109628

ISBN 0-9740909-4-8

FIRST EDITION

This book borrows. The author would like to acknowledge her debt to
the following authors: Pliny, Cotton Mather, Charles Olson, William
Carlos Williams, George Oppen, and lastly, Milbourne Christopher,
whose book, *Magic: A Picture History,* provided a wealth of information
on the nineteenth-century magicians who appear in this text. Thanks to
the Thompsons and the Alberta duPont Bonsal Foundation. Sincere
thanks to Claudia Keelan, Myung Mi Kim, and Graham Foust for their
careful and considerate readings. She extends her deepest gratitude to
Gordon Hadfield, her most constant editor, collaborator, and
companion.

CONTENTS

The notion of procuring *Invisibility* by any *Natural Expedient,* yet
known, is, I Believe, a meer *Plinyism;* How far it may be
obtained by a *Magical Sacrament,* is best known to the
Dangerous Knaves that have try'd it.

Cotton Mather

See how magic and the practice thereof is spread over the face
of the whole earth! . . . the benefit is inestimable that the world
hath received by the great providence of our Romanes, who
have abolished these monstrous and abominable arts.

Pliny

and a great gaping

                                     the compass of our knowledge

                   wound

                      around our ears

             k   nell   t

                   lull

                           a

                              peers

                   through

                   no relation

a

bye

lulla

lulla   lullaby

never harm nor spell nor charm

grovel

ERRAND #1

Make it the land of a thousand dies.
Make it colorful and unmatched.
Make it there and make it home.
Do not make it your own.
Make it in the manner of the old.
Make it only with the well-known.
Make it boast of its self.

Pliny indulges in lamentation for "the maner of the world in these our daise": "Full well I know, that I for my part also, shall have but small thanks for all my paines taken in writing this history of the world and Nature of works: Nay, I am assured that I make my selfe a laughing stocke, and am condemned of them for spending and losing my time in such a frivolous piece of worke as this is."

IN THESE OUR DAISE

do we know full well that it makes itself to boast of its self
or that we make it to boast of ourselves
or that we make it to boast of it
or that it makes us to boast of its self
or that it makes us to boast of ourselves,
and if so, could we safely say
we are still sages and wizards and witches?
Cuckoos or Davenport brothers. Boys from Buffalo.

IN VISIBILITY

numerous
find in our weeds
a sufficient history

and an ancient
invisibility
among our leaves

ERRAND #2

Run in/over and see what you can
and, of course, cannot

(the devil was Exceedingly Disturbed)

See.

This sixteenth-century time disturbed.

Securing skins and sacks of corn and seeds, knowing not whether they would be sown or stolen or simply abandoned, they proceeded further from shore. One sack of seeds so small nearing invisible, and some argued, not worth carrying since a seed so small would yield only little fruits. Small fruits of force: grapes, berries,

Conceal: seal and carry close, as in a pocket or a mind.
Or in the thickest spot of a raspberry bush to which one intends
to return.

ERRAND #3

Defy the gales and sail as close as the shoal will allow.
Whose boats did they secure? Disturb the devil
exceedingly and point to his invisibility.
Then, of course, return with riches.

Little clocks tick softly
into one
the say-fish bridles
violence and cleaves,
staying the ship.
The magic of small fish.

EQUALS ZERO

Being allowed to pass. The transportation fare, which, in this city, takes you from one no where to another no where, will be raised by the sum of one dollar in the coming year. The train passes, the train derails, the passage cost lives and dollars. It pleased God to throw this one overboard and to overcharge the other. Thanks be.

lulla

lulla

lull

a bye

ERRAND #4

Sail (or sell or buy) as much of the shore as possible, or steal,
preferably steal. We were to become the biggest producers of steel
in the world, the biggest in a thousand senses. All of those
grandfathers worked in that big mirrored building to make sure I
could have my metal, which brings me to errand #4:
Make sure we are in a position to mettle.

The boys from Buffalo never referred to themselves as spiritualists, but the label suited them and their cabinet séances, so they didn't protest.

ERRAND #5

Ask the thousand questions that yield good-looking answers: Industry, Honesty, Utility and Resourcefulness, among others. Abundance comes to those who don't waste. Don't we want to be a plentiful People?

Found abundance.
Then.
Number Resourcefulness.
Number Industry.
Plentiful good-looking people
he has on the world.

Honestly, this is the sum to be found.

ERRAND #6

Inchantresses.
Tame trees with hortyards and their wonderful
prices, as in each leaf a fortune one continent could
never match. "And we talk about the wilderness
with affection. We are blind asses, with our whole
history unread before us and helpless if we read it."
Coming early or coming late, being hurtful to all,
better we go and return with logs before
the fall of conjurers all together.

(and queer doings)

The Davenport Brothers, mediums not conjurers, the Boys from Buffalo, made
musical instruments levitate. During their shows in England, the boys were
accused of trickery, which they attributed to "professional jealousy, religious
prejudice and anti-American feelings."

Errand #7

Yankee swindle. During the swearing-in process,
levitate your own hands and lies are no longer lies,
but levities. The ties that/ the political bands that/
which have connected/ which do affiliate/
which provide assistance in/ which make us
of a common heritage/ which establish an allegiance/
are a swindling, and the trees sway, as in the maples
need milking and the tobacco, harvesting.
Hatchet a head, if need be.

Thanks be too. How many heads were hatcheted? How many hatched? A
new head began to appear where the old had been removed. A magician
who not only removed but replaced was sorely needed. But replaced with
a new head, a cross-pollinated, across lines of all sorts. Five shafts of
Cham's wit directed against the Davenport Brothers and their cabinet
séances. We want it open. We want it in mid-air, not behind doors,
cabinets or even windows, in mid-air like the Fowles.

OF THE CUCKOW:

"The reason why they would have other birds to sit upon their eggs and hatch them, is because they know how all birds hate them: for even the very little birds are readie to war with them: for feare therefore that the whole race of them should be utterly destroied by the furie of others of the same kind, they make no nest of their owne (being otherwise timorous and fearefull naturally of themselves) and so are forced by this craftie shift to avoid danger."

The Titling deceived sitting and hatching another bird's egg.

Surely He will save us from the fowler's snare.
Changelings do not record their history carefully,
surely we have been saved
from ourselves in this sense,
a nation of fowler's snares,
a nation of changelings,
but unaware
of being
either a nation of fowler's snares
or a nation of changelings.
The rest, which are her own indeed, she sets no store by,
as if the nation were a notion of changelings.

Whensoever at any time the changelings' parents are upon their
remove and departure, they persuade other birds to beare them
company. The birds who accompany are:

Orty go metra	the quail mothers, another name for the Landrail;
Glottis	a kind of plover;
Otis	the great bustard;
Cyc ram as	probably the ort olan;
Like-owl	bubo, a horned owl;
Howlet	a night owl

But the Titling, deceived, sitting and hatching another bird's egg.

ERRAND #8

There may be many orphans.
They may be made to join a magic act,
traveling and consorting
with the most questionable
of characters. You may be
called upon to redeem them,
but they have no hope, even in you.

In old time Magicke bare a great sway
and witches still swarm too much,
roasting herbs and simples.

Simply said, witches sway Magicke
and old times swarm still,
bare herbs and much roasting.

Of Clothes died with certain Herbs:
    Fairly said simply
    Purple of Tyrus
Scarlet and Violet of Graine
        reproduced
with the juice of only certain herbs

with a deepe blindness
these baies go unexplored
until word of gold
until wiser men ♣

make

other nations, not lives,
but stranger bodies sound and search
shell-fish,
the monstrous Whale of the Sea
or
wiser prey

our coasts have been rid of trickery
such as clothes died with certain herbs

♣ These men are wiser than their neighbors of other nations before them because:
1. They don't hazard themselves to search the bottom of the deep sea for Burrets, Purples, and shell-fishes.
2. They don't adventure their lives in strange coasts and blind bays.
3. They don't offer their bodies as prey for the monstrous whale of the sea.

When the Davenport brothers, boys from Buffalo, masters of the cabinet séance, created a sensation in Europe, Robin, famous French magician, insisted that the Davenports' tricks had nothing to do with the conjuring of spirits. He easily duplicated the Davenports' mysterious manifestations. He moved into. He made or didn't make or showed that the Davenports had never made or at the very least had made something other, something less authentic, than they had proposed to make.

ERRAND #9

Move into.
Choose a house you like, and move in.
Move right in.
No worries if someone lives there, take their room.
Pull your car into their garage,
and pen your dog up in their back yard.
Most importantly, pick the lemons their ancestors
have been growing for generations, search their
pantry for their sugar and make a sweet beverage.

A matter of right, religious or otherwise, permits
you to make invisible centuries-old inhabitants.

Some Americans claimed not to like the conjurers or the establishments in which they conjured. John Woolman, the great Quaker, insisted that the art of magic was of no use to the world. Where the devil dances on stilts to the tune of a hand organ. But even George Washington was a conjuring fan. The art of now-you-see-it-now-you-don't became firmly established as part of American life.

Seeming

                                                                    Impossibilities

seeds   mend

                                                        possible

           abilities   ancestors

posse   me   posit   seeds   fruit

     fruit   before   seeds   sanction

                                    ties

               sing   sea   and

     talk make take   ties   levities and

                           séances

                                        so sorry I stole

our nest   orphan

                    See   siblings

in   high

               trees and lies   tress

          you've

                                        talked to me like

               I've torn my dress

ERRAND #10

bring their hands together
who is caught red-handed
who has lain theirs
haul them up
haul them in
run away
come away

music and a song: sing within

Disaster of Doing

the magic scrapbook
has been overturned
and mighty heaps
cast out of hiding

In another place, the course and channel of rivers is turned clean away
and forced backward:
backward, the river is forced in another place
and clean channel (of) course is turned away.

The earth is sometimes knit together again, sometimes left wide open,
sometimes somewhat open, somewhat closed, sometimes open and
then closed, closed and then re-

-opened.

ERRAND #11

Climb to the top.
Let it come down.
Hear the flock of birds take off at once.
Hundreds, and imagine it as an earthquake
in reverse. The sky shakes and we dig
shelters over fault lines. We imagine
a reverse to let it come down and climb
to the top: stationary, traverse, torn through,
sit still, build a nest in the center
of the mountain, between an altitude
of snow and an altitude of sand,
at the level where one can see both seas.
See, this is not mine.

The sounds Pliny identifies:
　　lowing and bellowing of beasts
　　man's voice
　　clattering and rustling of armor and weapons
　　hollow cranes within
　　cranny by which it passeth
　　slender and whistling
　　tender and whistling ♣

♣ These noises are often heard without a quake.
I myself know for certain that the desert is a common place for quakes, that Pliny would
have believed the United States a common place for quacks, magicians.

ERRAND #12

Is "Earth's veins" accurate?:
Earthdin. Those things both tokens.
Afterward, many new springs discovered
elastic compression in any direction
springs sprung up in the ward,
       after:
see where the horsetempest becomes visible,
       earthquake?
Precipice, path, quake, road,
river, stationary, sanctuary, etc.

Several women have made earthquake
gowns, that is, warm gowns to sit
out of doors all night
tonight (an earthquake having been

       predicted). Make an earthquake gown,
       and don't tare.

A new spell:
legs shaky,
less strong,
legs long,
(let him feel
like a newborn
bird), have
queer round
and round
earth
after he leaves
the ward, have
him quaky
sort of feeling
earthquaky
very and
very.

Your vessels and your spells provide.

Dishes and such things as stood upon shelves come crashing to clatter//
afraid to go out of house, afraid of the house, afraid of the fear he felt,
afraid of the ground, afraid of the sky// as I've said it was almost in
reverse, afraid of the land, and of the water, because under the water, of
course, and afraid of the course he was told to take to avoid the greater
part of the disaster, and afraid of the disaster, the lesser and the
greater// he goes to see a spiritual advisor:

ERRORS IN #'S

One and nine
make
it one and ten
make it quietly
and without disturbance or
disaster
or bifarious bones or errand
or rupture or embarrassment

I've fortune-told you
        misfortune-told you

grown   together

  gown   gather

    showing   garter

      through   a tare

        or *for*   or *be*

          a   dear

           and sew a dress, sow a seed we can all

                                                                   wear

A MISFORTUNE

She hatched an imperfect baby, that's true.
When onlookers were told that other onlookers had already described
the baby's monstrosities, these accounts followed:

The baby was of normal size.
Though it had no head, it had a face.
It had hands, but instead of fingers it had talons.
It had skin, but it was scaly.
Its ears were placed upon its shoulders.
It had horns, four on the top of its head.
Though it had no head, it had a face.
It had no hands, though it had fingers.
Even though everything else surrounding
was happening in the year 1964,
the birth actually occurred in 1972.
The nose hooked downward.
It had three mouths, each with its own tongue,
all of which were forked.
Its belly was where its back ought to be,
and its legs where its arms ought to be.
Though the pregnancy lasted only seven months,
it was obvious the mother
had been housing this abnormality
for fourteen years.
It had died before, in 1964.
It was buried after, in 1962.

The thirtieth booke speaketh of Magicke, and certaine medicines appropriat to the parts and members of *man*'s bodie.

Harry Kellar, born in Erie, Pennsylvania, was a member of the Davenports' Company. He learned *from* them how to *outmake* them. Of Kellar, a Chicago reviewer wrote: "Then this devil of a fellow gives you an intermission and comes at you again with a cabinet séance that would make the Davenport Brothers and Slade jump off the Board of Trade tower for very envy . . . If the baldheaded Kellar had lived in the time of Cotton Mather, there would have been roast conjurer on toast one day."

ERRAND #13

Sail as close as the shoal will allow
on barrels
oil our Once rock
over the seas in a

The master storyteller has fallen asleep, and when he wakes
he'll have no way of reporting what we've made off with.

We need not report barrels of oil,
                        the birthmark on our bellies shone through.

Though we spill it on our way out, he'll slip and knock his head,
causing a concussion.

Oilet, eyelet, eye, bud
Eye light, oilet.

The oil lettings,
public beheadings,
the woman who grew ten heads
where hers was removed
is this many witnesses
of the disaster of doing.

"The Expanding Die"
was sold to Mrs. Will Goldston, who later sold it to Houdini,
who left it to his brother Hardeen, whose poster featured a beheaded lady
with no hair but a beautiful body and "Once Seen—
                                        Never Forgotten"

                    The Once Stone
                from the urine of an Once
                        a Lynx,
                  covered with earth
                out of spite and envy of
                      humankind,
              that he should have no good by it,
                      they hold

                      it at bay.

Money from thin air has always intrigued audiences. Macaluso delighted Parisian theater-goers by plucking gold pieces from a candle flame, and the art of now-we-see-it-now-you-don't became firmly engrained in American consciousness.

In
visibility
In
the hole
In
position
In
the right

(A concussion, with memory loss.)

In
ability
In
let
In
posit
In
site
In range
In rage
In position

now-we-see-it-
now-you-don't

An oil pump in the distance resembles a man waving his arms, either for assistance, as in frantically, or hospitably, as in *finally, company.*

A bittern lands on his arm, on a down swing.

ERRAND #14

Turn lands on their legs
for energy, virtue, power.
Medicinal fountains,
the wonderful burning,
so many hundreds of years
of fire issuing forth in so many places,
the deadly damps and exhalations,
either sent out of the pits
when they are sunk
or assuming the position of the ground.
Present death in one place
to the birds only, in others
to all living creatures,
bittern.

no initiation of
a new kind of nation
in range

SPELLINGS

we weeds
and our history

But believe me, Man at man's hand receiveth most harme and
mischiefe.

In strides the wilderness makes towards us its own errands,
innumerable, unnumberable and in-

                                               -relatable

                                          to our own.

way-side
weeds divine

1735: birth of Philadelphia,

the first American conjurer
to appear in Europe

Memory of the soul's existence in scenes he had never seen,
or in scenes she had not herself constructed, being moved about.

ZEGNER
ACQUITTED

NEW YORK
PRINTER ACQUITTED
OF SEDITIOUS
LIBEL FOR PRINTING
ATTACKS ON THE
ROYAL GOVERNOR
AND HIS FACTION.

WEALTH DISTRIBUTION
IN COLONIAL PHILADELPHIA
Percentage of wealth held by the

	RICHEST 10%	POOREST 30%
1684-1699	36.4	4.5
1700-1715	41.3	4.9
1716-1725	46.8	3.9
1726-1735	53.6	3.7
1736-1745	51.3	2.6
1746-1755	70.1	1.5
1756-1765	60.3	1.1
1766-1775	69.9	1.0

Thus, widening the freedom of the press.

Leaves: Tush.
Take those trees away,
true, we don't touch them any longer.

We've said we must make
or must try to make
the supreme effort. What wood endures and continues always good

                                        rare
                                        what wood

                                        oaken for poisonings
                                        and ivy for tincture
a small dose to see what touching might allow or disallow, initiate or
inculcate

walking of spels and charmes,
we grew apart

once we were together, as land masses ought to be
and walking was easy

Atlantic is Atlantis
no magic

Philadelphia, where/in whom charmes converged ♦

♦ 1. He takes two ladies and sets them on their heads on a table. With their legs up, he then gives
them a blow, and they immediately begin to spin like tops with incredible speed, without either of
their dead-dresses raised by the pressure, or the falling of their petticoats, to the very great satisfaction
of all present.
2. He draws three or four ladies' teeth, makes the company shake them well together in a bag, and
then puts them in a little cannon, which he fires at the aforesaid ladies' heads, and they find their
teeth white and sound in their places again.

Professor HARRINGTON, whose name is as familiar as "Household Words," has steadily entertained the people of New England for over a QUARTER OF A CENTURY with his Wonderful Ventriloquial Powers and Magical Metamorphoses.

His letter of warning:
disappear
to where
you have shown
their language
is never-resting

                                           to

Earth or Land.
My Land.
New Ground.
Fields Worne out.
Trees.
Branch, Branches.
Leafe, leaves.
A root of Tree,
A River.
A Bridge.
A little River.
A little Rivulet.
A Spring.
Is there a Spring?
Is there a River?
Is there a Bridge?

So that I might not be the royal illusionist.

ERRAND #15

Take a shovel.

mounds and mines
an errand wrapped
among itself

weary of capitals excavated
or unexcavated but presumed. The lake dropped low
this year, and the chimneys appeared just above the surface
of the water, and froze.

we've been this year

                              to seventeen magic shows

The whole of these Extraordinary Performances concluding with the Acme of Natural Magic, Entitled on the Continent, the HARMLESS GUILLOTIN.

Professor Harrington,
Proprietor of the Old New,

      has the essential features necessary for an Entertainment "to please
all and offend none"—and so complete his identification
with the audience, the illusory effect of

an EVENING AT HOME
unimpared

          his powers—
Newspaper Critics, Ministers of the Gospel, and in fact *the entire public* having
asserted him incomparable!—even his professional rivals conferring upon him
the significant and appropriate title of "AUTOCRAT OF THE MAGIC TABLE."

ERRAND #16

So many children
are taken in
by grace
these days.
Take some in
to become prime movers
in political and magical circles.

Despite his grim appearance, in 1865 the *Boston Bee* called Jonathan
Harrington the funniest man alive

> we among his queens
> needed a good laught
>   hives
>   hides
> in 1865
> in the abandoned hole
> ha ha ha ha ha ha ha-ha
> ha ha ha ha ha ha ha-ha-ha

> and so complete his identification
> with the audience

And rect-
-angles

wrecked tangles
his city he made appear
in her hair, of trees

invisible
his appearance:

A Disaster

for example, the order that bees keepe in their worke:

They both foresee and also foreshew.
They take their repast together.
They wake one another and command one another to sleep.
They are charged in full by the means of their muffle, muzzle.
They make slow haste.
They mark and note the slow-backs.
They chastise them and later punish them with death.
They do these things by snatches, give over quickly.
They get caught in the sheep's wool, their wolf.
They are duped by the frog.
They carry forth their dead.
They cast, when the time comes, their hue.
They drive drones out of doors.

ERRAND #17

Bee six cornered
Six-timed
Spring-timed
Eat and labor alike
at the same hour

The(ir) world is black magic
The(ir) world is half magic

Even the ladies attempted the Davenports' act.
Nella Davenport, no relation to the brothers, was a so-called spirit-reader,
spirit-writer,

anti-spirit medium.

In waves, in passing, as an imitator, in heart, in heat, in the reader's best
interest, in hand:

Nella

spells synergy

in range
and the sea makes a second gulf

a

dis-

taster

The compass of our knowledge wound around our ears.
Magic of a needle,
walking where one shouldn't,
doing and dreaming a disaster,
paying to see a disaster undone, magically.
Before Ira Davenport died, he met Houdini.
That which exists outside profane time reoccurs and preoccurs.
Nests do and do not go unoccupied,
deserts do and do not remain unconquered,
west does and does not remain west.
         No more root in the deep world
         or in the mid-world.

and now the whole globe

                                    divided in three parts
is a kind of wild wart growing beneath this moss
outside profane time   and linen that will not
                                          burn in fire

our earth resembles a radish—all radishes breed and provoke passers

                              o eat them
                              o heat them in fire

                              thistles, tad-stools, and funghi
                              the utter of the Milky Way

come away
come away

Fence Books was launched in 2001 as an extension of **FENCE**, a biannual journal of poetry, fiction, art and criticism that has a mission to redefine the terms of accessibility by publishing challenging writing distinguished by idiosyncrasy and intelligence rather than by allegiance with camps, schools, or cliques. It is part of our press's mission to support writers who might otherwise have difficulty being recognized because their work doesn't answer to either the mainstream or to recognizable modes of experimentation.

THE ALBERTA PRIZE is an annual series administered by Fence Books in collaboration with the Alberta duPont Bonsal Foundation. The Alberta Prize offers publication of a first or second book of poems by a woman, as well as a five thousand dollar cash prize.

Our second prize series is the **FENCE MODERN POETS SERIES**. This contest is open to poets of either gender and at any stage in their career, and offers a one thousand dollar cash prize in addition to book publication.

For more information about either prize, visit our website at **WWW.FENCEBOOKS.COM**, or send an SASE to: Fence Books/[Name of Prize], 303 East Eighth Street, #B1, New York, New York, 10009.

For more about *Fence,* visit **WWW.FENCEMAG.COM**.

FENCE BOOKS TITLES

A MAGIC BOOK   Sasha Steensen
                                    2004 ALBERTA PRIZE

The Commandrine and Other Poems   Joyelle McSweeney

MACULAR HOLE   Catherine Wagner

The Opening Question   Prageeta Sharma
                              2004 FENCE MODERN POETS SERIES

Sky Girl   Rosemary Griggs
                                    2003 ALBERTA PRIZE

Nota   Martin Corless-Smith

APPREHEND   Elizabeth Robinson
                              2003 FENCE MODERN POETS SERIES

Father of Noise   Anthony McCann

The Real Moon of Poetry and Other   Tina Brown Celona
Poems   2002 ALBERTA PRIZE

The Red Bird   Joyelle McSweeney
                              2002 FENCE MODERN POETS SERIES

Can You Relax in My House   Michael Earl Craig

ZIRCONIA   Chelsey Minnis
                                    2001 ALBERTA PRIZE

MISS AMERICA   Catherine Wagner